THE ULTIMATE
PROJECT
MANAGER
GUIDE

Step-by-step guide to make you a superstar Project Manager

FAREED RAJA

Contents

CHAPTER ONE: INTRODUCTION

Welcome

Okay, so maybe you are embarking upon a brand new career in project management, or you are an existing project manager that is now looking to take their career to the next level. Whatever your starting point, this book will teach you how to manage your projects effectively from beginning to end. What is project management? The term is so broad and can be applied to so many aspects of business that a lot of people get confused by it. I will break it down into bite-sized, relevant chunks that you can then take away and apply. We will start with the nuts and bolts; the general concepts behind project management, before giving you the tools that you will need to a. Identify the problem and b. Work out what needs to be done to solve it. When you are comfortable with that, we will walk through planning your project, devising a schedule and setting the ground rules for how you want your project to be run. Finally, I'll give you a whole bunch of tried and tested tips not just for effectively launching your project, but crucially for monitoring its performance helping you stay on time and in budget. Who said project management couldn't be fun?!

Defining A Project

What use is a project manager without a project to manage? Once we have established the guidelines and defined "a project" we will run through the basics; the standard approaches to project management that you will use day in and day out. I will then help arm you with the skills and tools needed to manage them. It is worth remembering that while they may be similar, no two projects, or managers are the same. By taking the basics and injecting the wow factor you should end up with a smooth flowing project that exceeds all expectations.

What is a project? No, this is not a trick question. A project is unique. It has a clearly defined beginning and end, and there is usually a budget attached to it. Imagine that you have the blueprints for a new build house. You would probably assume that the work involved in putting the house together would be the same every single time. However, as with just about everything in life, unforeseen events, and circumstances can alter the process. The construction industry is full of variables. Someone might order the wrong sized sheets for the roof. Torrential rain might cause flooding in the foundations. Heavy snowfall could delay excavation. A good project manager will embrace this and accept that while there may be similarities, each new construction project is unique.

Now that you have identified your project, you need to set a clear goal. Using the house building project as an example. The goal may be to put up this house as part of a wider development. There might be financial penalties attached to the project if it is not completed on time. Your goal is, therefore, to get this house, and the rest in the development up on time. Easy, right? Yes, provided you get the next part right! It is crucial that your project has a clear beginning and end. You cannot allow a project like the one that I have just outlined to run on forever, or you will risk bankrupting either your company or your client's company. You have to start as you mean to go on, and make sure that small niggles don't turn into catastrophic problems. For a start, this means standing over your contractors with a stick if need be. If you do find that a project is dragging on, then you will need to revisit your final goal as it is possible that you haven't clearly defined it enough. "Budget" doesn't have to be a dirty word, but it can be if you don't stick to it. There is so much more to this beauty than just money. Time and resources need to be carefully managed otherwise you could end up a big, black hole in your budget that is impossible to bridge.

A lot of people confuse operations with project management. Operations are the processes that a company must go through on a daily basis in order to stay in business. Operations start on day one with the inception of the business and then run seamlessly like clockwork day in and day out. There is no end date and the budget is rolling. While operations might be run on an ad hoc basis in small businesses, most medium to large businesses would have an operations manager whose job was purely to oversee the smooth running of the day to day business. Let me give you an example to demonstrate, I used to be in charge of the technical support group of a software company. Our team opened and closed support requests on a daily basis. That is all they did. While each request was different and unique, the processes that we followed were the same. It was operational. However, I was also tasked with modifying our systems and harnessing our international offices with the view to the company providing 24-hour technical support to our clients. There was a goal with a beginning, end, and budget. This was a project.

Excellent organizational skills are a pre-requisite for anyone considering a career in project management. It is a very different skill set from say, for example, sales. Effective project management requires the ability to undertake tasks in a logical and methodical manner and the very fact that they are good at making things happen, is often the reason project managers land their first job. However, there is much more to this role than simply organizing the office and supervising staff. If you can answer the following two simple questions then you will be more than halfway there:

1. What is the problem that needs solving?
2. How are you going to solve the problem?

Get in the habit of repeating these two questions over and over, kind of like a mantra AND solving them, and the rest will pretty much fall into place. How to solve the problem can sometimes also be a minefield. For example, there might be several possible outcomes that all have their merits and initially seem viable. As a project manager, it is your job to walk mentally through each one, identifying the pitfalls, before reaching a decision as to the best way forward. There is no time for indecision. If you have carefully worked through all of your options, then the "How" should be easy enough to execute.

Formulating your plan

Once you know the route that you are going to take, you have to plan each and every step to ensure that you don't trip up or encounter difficulties along the way. Here are some important factors to consider:

- Compile a detailed breakdown of the work involved in the project.
- How long will the work take to complete?
- What resources do you need? How much do they cost?
- Define "success" – What will your project look like when it is complete? Every project is different, and therefore success is a chameleon. To return to my house-building example of earlier, success might take the form of an increase in sales, or it may be handing over the keys to the realtor.

Take some time out at the end of each project to ask yourself:

- How well did the project go?

Don't be tempted to skip this aspect; even if you feel that the project was a rip-roaring success. So, before you crack open the champagne and give yourself a congratulatory pat on the back take some quiet time out to contemplate what you could have done better. This will make you better at what you do, and help each project run more seamlessly than the last. There is also no point lying to yourself. Honest brutality is the key.

Understanding What It Takes To Be A Project Manager

If you were to ask the average person on the street about how they perceived a project manager, they would probably scratch their heads in bemusement for a moment or two, before answering that they are:

1. Organized.
2. Good at getting things done.

In reality, a project manager is a jack of all trades; the eternal juggler. When they first start their training, project managers must learn technical skills that are specific to project management. They need to learn:

- How to craft a formal project plan.
- How to build and then fine tune a schedule as the project is being rolled out.
- How to measure success using tools such as earned-value analysis.
- It is also that they learn how to ensure that a project delivers value for money for the client.

As I have already alluded to, you need to ensure that your project achieves the goals and objectives laid out at the start of the process. It is also imperative that you take the time to research and fully understand what makes your organization tick. You need to get to the very heart and soul of it so that you can make sure that the project is relevant. Rather than being the shy, retiring bean counting type. A project manager is at the very forefront of the action. They are the formula one drivers, steering the team to success. Strong interpersonal skills are critical.

Unfortunately, while these skills can often be fine-tuned and enhanced, it is very difficult to teach them from scratch. As a project manager, you will be liaising with people from all different backgrounds and walks of life. Everyone from directors to *secretaries*. You need people to *want* to walk that extra mile for you when the going is tough, rather than having to drag them by their shoelaces. If you can't motivate people, and struggle to inspire them, then getting your project to completion, on time and budget, is going to be at best an uphill struggle.

The Five Processes Of Project Management

There are five major processes that all project managers must follow day in and day out. The Project Management Institute classifies them as follows:

1. Initiating, or committing to a project. What is the problem? How are you going to solve that problem?

2. Planning. A detailed breakdown of how you intend to see the project through from beginning to end. What is the plan? How will you measure success or define completion?

3. Execution. This begins the very second that you launch our project. You recruit your team, a.k.a. "your resources," you introduce them to each other and quickly establish the ground rules.

4. Monitoring and control. This is an ongoing task that you must keep abreast of every single day. By keeping across your project, you will be aware of any little snags or glitches and be able to take steps to address them before they become a major problem for you. By ensuring that you never veer too far from your intended path, you greatly increase your chances of completing your project on time and budget. (See the recurring theme here!)

5. Finalizing your project. If you have done your job properly, then this part should be brief and enjoyable. Your client needs to confirm officially that the project has been completed to their satisfaction. As discussed earlier, you then formally document the overall performance of the project, and you take the time out to reflect on lessons learned and re-deploy your team to other assignments.

Traditional vs. Agile Project Management

I now want to walk through the two most common approaches to project management before showing you how to identify which method to adopt. Remember, each project is unique and what is best in one set of circumstances may prove catastrophic in others. You should now be completely familiar with the five processes involved in project management, and we are now going to consider what happens when each process flows smoothly, one after the other. Think of it as the stars being in perfect alignment, or the "waterfall approach" as it is commonly referred to. The "waterfall approach" a.k.a. Traditional project management works exceptionally well if you are relatively familiar with the project, there is a clearly identifiable goal, the result is easily achievable and you're totally comfortable with the tools and technology that you are using. In other words, when you are in your comfort zone and you could manage the project in your sleep.

Unfortunately, most of the projects that you get assigned are vastly different. You don't have a clue what the result looks like and so while winging it is an absolute non-starter in project management, you do still have to figure it out and adapt as you go along. In order to pull this off you are going to have to step WAY out of your comfort zone and adopt a completely different approach. I like to think of agile project management as a seductive little dance that gradually moves you closer to your goal. For example, your goal might be to replace an outdated financial system with a more efficient, streamlined version. However, your client may have neglected to document his existing procedures and requirements. So, thinking back to our seductive little dance where we gradually work our way closer and closer to our goal, instead of visualizing the end goal, we must also visualize each step.

While this undoubtedly requires a far higher level of brainpower and maneuvering, you might be pleasantly surprised to find that the process of implementing the project is a lot easier. This is because Agile projects typically require small teams of highly skilled people who rather than being scattered around the four corners of the world, are conveniently based in the same location. Therefore, it is easier to keep everyone on track, and troubleshoot. You will also be obsessing and picking over the tiniest detail of the project in a way that wouldn't be necessary with traditional project management. Which means that any problems will be identified and addressed almost as soon as they have occurred.

Exploring Project Management Software Options

Advances in technology mean that there is now a vast array of software options at your disposal. Choose wisely, and your job as a project manager will be so much easier. I am going to walk you briefly through some of the most popular options:

Different Types Of Software

There is no one size fits all with scheduling software as it comes in the whole spectrum of shapes and sizes. If your project is relatively simple, then you might just want to use spreadsheet to determine which team members will work on what tasks on any given day. However, for larger or more complex projects then trusted programs such as Project and Primavera will probably best meet your needs. Both of these programs come with a mind-blowing array of features that will assist in setting up and managing your project's schedule. If the price of these programs is going to wreck your budget before you even get started on your project, then there are other options, FastTrack Schedule, OpenProj and @Task all immediately spring to mind. If you sit back and think about the many documents that will be produced during the lifetime of a project, then you will quickly come to the conclusion that a word processing program is essential. As we have already discussed, while no two projects are the same, many are similar. It makes sense to create templates of documents to avoid having to start from scratch every time. Remember, managing time is critical to delivering the project in budget. Having a spreadsheet program will also make complex analysis and calculations. For example, a spreadsheet could be used to analyze potential risks and prioritize the most likely.

Everyone has heard of PowerPoint, but how many project managers automatically add it to their "must have" list? Presentation programs such as this can be a lifesaver when having to communicate important information about your project at a senior level. You will also need a tool to make collaborating with others easier. Basecamp and Microsoft SharePoint are useful on several different levels. Not only do they enable you to share files with others, but critically, they can even help you manage your workflow.

Finally, there is Enterprise-level software. You will only need this if you work on very large projects, or your organization has dozens of projects running simultaneously. This incredible software provides tools that help you build a team with the exact skill set that you need for your project. It will save you a lot of time and effort, filtering out unsuccessful candidates. It also helps you track risks and build document libraries so that your team members can access the information that they need at the click of a mouse. While this software is expensive, if the cost is absorbed in multiple projects then there are savings in terms of time to be made.

Choosing the right software for *you* and *your* project is going to be a deeply personal decision. It will depend upon a number of factors, including your particular technical skillset and the degree that you are already comfortable with certain software. It will also depend on the number of other projects that you manage, as well as their complexity.

CHAPTER TWO: INITIATING A PROJECT

Initiating a Project

Whether this is your first or fiftieth project, starting a new one is always an exciting and nerve-wracking time. You will be bursting with ideas and full of hope for the weeks and months that lie ahead. However, from a practical point of view, the aim of the initiating process, rather than being some kind of ritual as the term suggests, is actually to gain a solid commitment from the management team to commence. You want the go-ahead. This is your chance to not only clearly identify and define the problem/task that your project will resolve, but also compile and present a project definition, or product summary.

You might find that he project has already been approved before you are even assigned as project manager. However, just so that you are fully equipped to deal with any scenario that might arise, I am going to run through the key elements of a project summary. I will also show you how to identify stakeholders in your project and the best way to present it in order to increase your chances of approval.

Writing a Problem Statement

In previous sections, we covered the need to ensure each project has a specific goal. Remember, it is that goal that drives every decision within a given project and so must be described in detail. However, with goals, comes the need to identify the problems that may hinder achievement and this is known as a Problem Statement. Unlike goal setting, problem statements do not have to be laborious in detail but moreover, should be succinct and attention grabbing. After all, your clients and stakeholders are incredibly busy people.

Let's take a look at an example:

Your client has three hundred employees and is looking to bring in another hundred in order to meet a certain objective. The problem that they would be facing in this instance is the lack of space in the current office which has a maximum capacity of three hundred and twenty people. To communicate this in a nice succinct way, you could simply say 'we don't have enough space for all of the employees'. That's it – a nice and simple statement that requires no further explanation.

It is important that the statement remains as a problem to be solved with no identified solution. This is easier than it sounds, because people generally want to find a solution when presented with a problem and this can often be a tricky area for new project managers to adhere to but it does get easier with practice. The quickest way to learn this technique is to question 'why' every time you think that a potential solution is being offered. So in the example above, the obvious solution to the problem would be to say 'we need a new building'. As the project manager you need to be able to challenge this pre-emptive thinking by asking 'why' and you should keep doing this until you are completely satisfied with the answer being given. In this way, you will ensure that all areas and options are fully explored before reaching a specific and clearly identifiable objective.

Defining Project Goals & Objectives

Okay, so you should by now be crystal clear as to what you need to do in order to define your project. You now need to describe precisely what the project is supposed to achieve. Lay out a project goal. In other words, the high-level target that you are aiming for as an outcome. In the same way that your problem statement needs to be concise, the same applies here. You need to come up with a simple statement that is clear, unambiguous, and easy to understand. You will then run with this and use it as means of getting your team to buy into the project and gently guide them to a successful conclusion. This could be achieved with say a corporate sales event.

Objectives are an excellent means of defining the goal even further by fleshing out specific details. Clearly identified objectives are crucial, in that they enable you to define not just the scope, but also the approach that you are going to adopt as well as the criteria upon which success will be measured. Business objectives are usually strategies or tactics that support the goal of the organization. For example, the objective might be to reduce the return rates on orders. This will then feed into the overall goal that each project should deliver a fifteen percent return on the money invested in the project.

Quality objectives will always place an exact figure on expected results. For example, if the goal of your project is to increase levels of customer satisfaction, you are going to need to increase the number of customer satisfaction ratings. Sometimes people's barriers shoot up, and they shy away from technical objectives. However, a good project manager will always embrace them. A prime example of this would be if you need to use robust machinery that is designed to withstand extreme conditions and harsh environments. Objectives may also fall into the catch-all bracket of performance. Think about it, performance can mean, or be attached to just about anything. An example of, when this might come into play, would be if your project needed to finish by a specific date, like say, a product release date.

Okay, so now that you are comfortable with objectives. What about document objectives? If you are formally documenting something, then it is imperative that your communications are clear in order to prevent any misunderstanding. Vague, flaky, objectives are no use to anyone as the likelihood of them getting you what you want is negligible. A good example of a specific written objective would be "We need to host an event that not only reaches eighty percent of our customer base, but also costs no more than $80,000."

When you are writing your objective, remember to make sure that they are measurable. What is the point of setting an objective that no-one is going to be able to measure? Your organization needs to know what went well, and what didn't. The only way that they are going to be able to do this is if the objective is measurable. For instance, ratings from surveys can be used to measure customer satisfaction. Realistic objectives also spell out what you can do with the resources available. There is a fine balance between setting challenging objectives can motivate people, and unrealistic objectives that will only serve to demoralize people. Time-related objectives identify when they can expect to be achieved. For example, a new product might need to be available in stores before the end of the year.

The key to time-related objective is always to ensure that you set a clear target date. Don't be tempted to cop out by setting a flimsy provisional date, say June/July. Be specific. If you commit, then your team will too. Referring back to the problem statement that you wrote earlier as a guide, now write a project goal. Remember that this must state your anticipated result. Keep it short, simple, and easy for everyone to understand. Then write your objectives, keeping them specific, measurable, realistic, and time-related.

Choosing a Strategy

Once you have your goal and objectives, chances are you are going to realize quickly that there is more than one possible strategy that you can adopt. Choice is a great thing, but it can also very quickly box you into a corner unless you remain focused. As a project manager, one of your core responsibilities is thoroughly to evaluate the pros and cons of alternative strategies before choosing the best solution, and this is when having great interpersonal skills will come into play. Gather together the most trusted members of your team and invite them to join with you in brainstorming potential strategies. As a group, you should read the problem statement, the goal, and the objectives and then start generating strategies. Don't inhibit the group by placing unnecessary restrictions on them. Ensure that they are relaxed and at ease, and encourage a free flow of ideas. Your aim is to get as many ideas down on paper as possible (before you begin picking them apart or evaluating them). Once you have a list, and you are ready to begin the evaluation process, I would recommend using a decision matrix to compare and contrast all of your options. As a group, you need to discuss how well the strategy satisfies the objectives of the project. The best way of quickly narrowing down your list is to check whether a particular strategy satisfies all of the must-have objectives and eliminate any that don't. Rate the performance of each objective for the strategies that passed the initial cut. If some objectives are more important than others, increase the credence that you give to them. The winner should be the strategy with the overall rating. It is not exactly rocket science; it is simply a process of elimination.

Then, your group needs to consider whether the chosen strategy is feasible. For example, you may find that strategies that are heavily reliant on new technology or unproven methods may not be as effective as you would hope. If you ascertain that feasibility might be an issue, then you may wish to consider a feasibility study to determine whether or not it will work without wasting too much time or resources.

If the feasibility could be an issue, a feasibility study can explore whether this strategy will work without committing too much time or money. Third, you need to consider whether the risks of this strategy are acceptable? You are not a magician, and it is impossible to be aware of all of the risks at this stage of a project. However, you can perform an initial risk analysis to see whether any risks are so significant and likely that you don't want to proceed. Fourth, ask does this strategy fit the culture of the organization? Trying to impose a strategy that doesn't fit with the culture within an organization is a losing battle, and you will not be able to bring either the management or your team with you. Always remember that the strategy that you choose has to satisfy most if not all of the project objectives. As soon as you choose a solution from your list of alternative strategies then the details of your project should start falling seamlessly into place.

Gathering Requirements

The goal, objectives, and solution for a project sets out what you are trying to achieve and the path that you intend taking to get you there. Requirements are the blueprint for the outcome and set out the specific needs of the project. This is an important process that must not in any circumstances be overlooked. If, for whatever reason, you end up failing to identify the requirements properly then your client will not be satisfied with the overall results of the project. It might sound like a no-brainer, but you would be surprised at how many project managers neglect to give this the due diligence that it deserves. Likewise, if you add in unnecessary requirements, then the project will inevitably take longer and cost more than it should.

Let's think for a moment or two about corporate sales events. One objective might be to showcase both new and existing products. A key requirement could be to include all the selling points that the sales team identifies in each presentation. Another requirement could be to use the organization's brand terminology in all presentations. These requirements are both necessary and detailed. Gathering requirements can be challenging. Sometimes customers know what they want and sometimes they don't and it is your job as the project manager to gently coax this information out of them.

Customers and stakeholders often confuse items that they have on their wish-list with true requirements. A good project manager will be able to keep drilling down until they have a detailed understanding of what it is that their client needs. You also need to be wary of people who have no stake whatsoever in your project who will for one reason or another try and hijack your services and add their wants and needs onto your list. As the project manager, it is your responsibility to be able to distinguish between true requirements and faux requirements, and politely spell out the boundaries. There are several tried and tested techniques that you can use when gathering requirements. As with most things in business, there are pros and cons attached. I know that I keep harking back to this, but you need to bear in mind that every project is unique and therefore requirements are going to differ according to the project that you are undertaking. Each technique has its pros and cons. If your current project is very similar to one that you have successfully undertaken in the past, there is no harm in starting with those requirements and then tweaking them accordingly.

In order to do this, you will need all of the documentation from the earlier project. You will need to scrutinize each document with a fine toothcomb, and ascertain whether certain features have become obsolete and whether new ones are now available. A great and fun way of fleshing out requirements is to build a prototype. This is usually a quick and rough model that your clients can use to test drive an idea. It is perfect in situations where they are not entirely certain about what they want.

Be Prepared!

Be prepared for the fact that you might have train people on the methodology that you are going to be using, or that you may have to hire people that are experienced with the tools and equipment. If your project involves several different groups, then don't be afraid to hold requirements meetings with representatives from each group to discuss their requirements for the project. These meetings not only help identify specific business needs but are advantageous in sense that they offer up a perfect opportunity to get people from the attending departments on board in a way that wouldn't have been possible without the actual meeting. If your audiences are vastly different, then it may be wise to hold different meetings to cater for them. For example, the requirements of the I.T. department will probably be very different from those of finance. You might even go as far as to have one group attend as observers: so that they can form an understanding of the requirements of other groups.

Observe With Sensitivity

If the goal of your project is to change the working environment of a particular department then it can sometimes be a good idea to observe people in the workplace: watch what people do in the course of their day-to-day activities. Don't go charging in like a bull in a china shop. Think this through and be aware that the mere act of being observed can make people feel uncomfortable and ill at ease. It can sometimes also lead to them behaving in an unnatural way. Sensitivity is the key to observation.

Make sure that they understand that you are there to help them and make their working conditions better, rather than make their lives harder. Ask them for their input; their thoughts on what could be better and how things can be improved. Make a note of their comments for reference.

Interview, Don't Interrogate

Informally interviewing people can also be a great way of identifying requirements. This is slightly more structured than a casual observation, and you would go into this armed with a list of pre-prepared questions. It is vital though that you put the person that you are interviewing at ease and that you get them to buy into your overall vision. By having a standard list of questions, you can be certain that you are asking everyone the same questions, and this will avoid anything being left out. Once this process has been completed, you can then document your requirements by writing detailed statements as to what needs to be completed in the project in order to satisfy the objectives.

Understanding Deliverables & Success Criteria

People expect to see something tangible at the end of a project. Concrete proof that it has been completed. These are broadly referred to as deliverables and refer to the final product. Deliverables come in all shapes and sizes and might be a building, software, or a new employee. Other times deliverable are more abstract, like a new service. During the planning process having deliverables in mind will help define the project scope; an understanding of what is, and is not included in the project.

Once your project gets underway, deliverables are a brilliant measure of progress. Write a list of the deliverables at the beginning of the project. Start at the end and work backward. So, start with the goods or services that your project will deliver upon completion. For example, if your project were to organize a corporate sales event then the result would be to print one thousand sales brochures to be distributed at the event. Then, document your intermediate deliverables: the items or services that will be delivered at various different stages throughout the project. So for example, assuming that the end deliverable was to print one thousand sales brochures, and then an intermediate deliverable might be to sign a contract with the printing company. Remember, that because they relate to the smooth running of the project, and then the intermediate deliverables are frequently for your eyes only. With that in mind, and so that you can keep your client fully in the loop at all times, it is wise to try and establish key deliverables that can be achieved in the time between sending status reports. This way both you and the client will be able to evaluate progress based upon the most recent status report. If your deliverable is too big, then you might feasibly end up going months with nothing tangible to show, which could easily result in a jumpy client. Always break your deliverables down into manageable pieces.

How do you know if you have got what you asked for?

Now that you know exactly what your deliverables are and at which stage of the project you will receive them, you might be wondering how you will know if what you get, is actually what you wanted? It is vital that you have some means of measuring them. In this scenario, success is all about criteria. Some are incredibly easy to work out. For example vendor contracts or the certificate of occupancy for a building. However, other criteria is often a lot harder to measure. So, in order to be effective in your role you always need to write success criteria that that is clear and quantifiable.

Going back to the example of the corporate sales event. Your definition of success might be the number of customers who attend. The number of products that are sold at the event or a high rating on a survey about the likelihood of attendees purchasing your products or services in the near future

Identifying Assumptions & Understanding Risks

You MUST protect your project and your plan by identifying assumptions and potential risks from the word go. Making assumptions is something that we are all guilty of in our day to day lives; presuming something to be true without independently verifying it. We are all different, and so the scope for assumptions is enormous. If they are not identified and thrashed out right at the start, then I can guarantee that someone, somewhere is going to end up disappointed. For example, if you assume that the marketing department will send out invitations to customers and marketing in turn assumes that sales will carry out that task. Then there is a strong probability that you won't realize until it is too late, and you could have a disaster on your hands when the invitations fail to be sent out and no one shows up!

Assumptions are often very difficult to identify. You can't see them, or feel them, and people often don't even realize that they are making one. The key is to delegate all tasks so that someone owns every last detail. One way of ensuring that there are no sneaky assumptions lurking around waiting to wreak havoc upon your project is to ask questions every step of the way. Don't be afraid of asking the same question over and again, until you are satisfied. Think of routing out assumptions as going undercover or being a detective. By asking the same question over and again, you will quickly sense when the story changes. Ask everyone what results they expect to see. Ask them to define success. This will help you marry everything up. If the list that you come up with exceeds budget or available resources, then a frank discussion with the team should help you bring it all back under control.

Defining the risk

In project management terms, a risk is a situation or an event that is likely to impact negatively on your project. Risks are events that may or may not arise but will cause problems if they do occur. You need to spend time during the early stages of your project scouring for risks. This will give the management team the opportunity to make an informed decision about whether or not to invest in the project. If you identify several alarming risks, it might be better to forgo the project in favor of another one.

By documenting assumptions and risks, while you flesh out the shape of your project will enable the management team to consider the viability before giving approval and proceeding to the planning stage.

Creating a Scope Statement

Once you have documented your project requirements and deliverables, you will need to create a scope statement that will outline the project in detail and also outline the boundaries for the project. Your scope statement will:

- Clearly state what is and is not included.
- Help you evaluate whether the project is performing as projected.

Let's use the corporate sales event as an example again. Your statement should:

- Identify which team is responsible.
- Indicate any out of scope work, i.e. work that is beyond the remit of the team.

If the trade show organizers are responsible for running the electrical service and delivering your shipment to your booth on the trade show floor then your scope should clearly identify what your team is expected to do and what the trade show people will do.

The out-of-scope section is a good place to document assumptions about what is outside the boundaries of your project. A scope statement is also brilliant at preventing a project expanding. Follow it to the letter, and it will not only help ensure that you deliver the overall project within budget but also help you dodge Scope creep; a hazard that many project managers fail to prevent happening. It is very easy for customers and team members to come up with little "add-ons." As soon as you become aware of this happening you need to nip it politely in the bud. It is, after all, YOUR responsibility as the project manager to deliver within budget and on time. If someone has a good case for adding something on, then you can discuss it and decide whether or not it is viable. Because a scope statement defines the boundaries of a project at a high level, you also need a change-management process to control the smaller change requests as and when they come in. I will be discussing this further in the next chapter.

Identifying Stakeholders

Sometimes, it can be difficult to determine just exactly who your stakeholders for your project are. Put simply, a stakeholder is someone who has a 'stake' in the outcome of your project. This includes customers, internal departments that are affected by your project and of course those who are working on specific project related tasks. In order to identify your stakeholders, you need to ascertain the major stakeholder roles, as follows:

- The person or group with the problem to solve: This is your **customer** and as well as supplying the project funding, they also provide input as to what the project will do and approve the deliverables.

- The person or group who want to see the project succeed and have enough formal authority to help make is happen: This is your **sponsor** and as well as helping to prioritize objectives, they can also talk to unsupportive stakeholders and suggest improvements to the plan.

- The person or group who run departments and are accountable for achieving their department's goals: This is your **functional (or line) manager** and they also manage the people within their departments; the very people that you need to make your project a success.

- The person or group that are working with you on the delivery of your project: This is your **team member** and as their jobs depend on how well they perform their specific assignment, it is important that they remain motivated to ensure that the project is successful.

Once you have identified all of your major shareholders, the next task becomes one of forging strong working relationship with all of them. To do this, you need to get to grips with what motivates them and adapt your style accordingly. It is also important to understand how they are connected to your project and what influence they have over the outcome. It may also be prudent to determine who the stakeholder listens to and this could be a valuable insight should a problem arise that you need help with.

As well as ensure excellent verbal communication, you should also ensure that you utilize written documentation. One way to keep track of everything is to store all of your information in a stakeholder analysis document. This should include the department, business unit or company that your stakeholder belongs to as well as their contribution to the project. This will help to ensure that you know what to expect from each stakeholder and also who to turn to for specific thing that you might need.

Obtaining Approval

Okay, so now that you have defined the project, you now have the task of seeking approval from the stakeholders in order to proceed with planning. Obtaining approval is important because you need commitment from project stakeholders to make a project a success. There are several ways of seeking approval:

Email

You might choose to mail or email a letter to the stakeholders asking them to sign on the dotted line. However, I do not think that this is the best approach to take. Yes, they might very well put their name to the project, but in the event of disagreements later down the line, they can easily disappear, and you end up back at square one.

Face-to-face sign off meeting

This is much more effective. Arrange a meeting with the sole aim of obtaining approval. The agenda is uncomplicated. Simply review the project summary and ensure that the stakeholders are in agreement. Deal with any issues as they arise, if the issues are too large then you may have to reschedule while you go back and rework the documents. Once everyone is happy simply get them to sign, and you are done and dusted!

Video conference or conference call

This is ideal if it is impossible to get everyone together in the same room. People in other locations can simply send you the signed documentation via email, fax or snail mail if necessary. Remember, a project summary is not a legally binding document. Make sure that your stakeholders are aware that you are not going to bankrupt them over this. The important thing is that the stakeholders fully understand what the project entails and that they buy into it.

Writing a Project Charter

As a project manager, you are only assigned a level of authority for the duration of the project and as such, do not have the kind of authorities that are given to other types of managers that work within a structured organization. This does also have the added advantage of affording you an objective view and protecting you from the inevitable office politics that are likely to ensue.

One of your tasks as project manager is to ensure that everyone involved (i.e., the stakeholders) have a clear understanding of what exactly your remit is and where your authority starts and finishes. As this can be critical to project success, it is recommended that this is formally documented in the form of a Project Charter.

Your Project Charter should include the following:

- Name of the project.
- Purpose of the project – a single sentence covering the summary objective will suffice.
- Name of the project manager.
- Responsibilities of the project manager.
- Extent of the authority of the project manager.
- Specific work to be performed by the project manager (signing contracts).

This document, once finalized, forms the agreement between the project manager and the customer and/or sponsor and should be circulated to all stakeholders. This is commonly carried out by the sponsor (as a show of support and endorsement of the project manager) and tends to be via email.

Once this step has been completed, everything will be in place to proceed to the planning process.

CHAPTER THREE: PLANNING A PROJECT

Planning A Project

It is during the planning process that you will identify what must be done, who is going to do it, how long it will take, when things will happen, and how much it will cost. You also need to plan in detail how you will run the project. Things to consider at this stage are:

1. Methods of communication.
2. Managing change and risk.
3. Quality control.

This all gets documented and when pulled together formulates your plan. You will refer back to the plan on a daily basis when the project gets underway. You will do this in order to:

- Give direction to those working on your project.
- Keep a track of the project.
- Alter course if needed.
- Communicate with team members and management.

Understanding Work Breakdown Structures

One of the most important tools that a project manager can utilize is a Work Breakdown Structure, commonly referred to as the WBS. The reason it is so important? Firstly it is a great way to break down the key components of a project into manageable sections and in doing so, provides the best way to manage the budget and timing. Secondly, by having specific elements of the project documented in a structured way, you can more easily assess progress and quickly identify any sticking points that may or may not lead to an overall delay to the completion of the project itself.

As you might expect, the WBS allows you to lay out the requirements of the project from the simplest to the most complex of tasks. This has the added benefit of helping you to see who within the team is best suited to each individual project – both in terms of workload and skills match. Hopefully, now you can see why the WBS is considered to be the most important of all the tools that a project manager has available to them.

Of course the number of layers in your WBS very much depends on the complexity of your project to begin with. For example something relatively straightforward like hosting an event will not be anywhere near as detailed as a WBS for the introduction of a new car model. In essence, the WBS lets you map out all the details of your project from the highest to the lowest level so would include things such as the steps needed to get to the stage of printing some new marketing material for example.

Now that you know what a WBS is and why it is so valuable, the next stage is to learn how to construct one for yourself – don't worry it is not as difficult as it sounds.

Building a Work Breakdown Structure

The best way to build a WBS is to start at the top and work your way down. By top, I mean the top level of summary tasks. For larger projects, it is often better to work as a team and initially identify the top two levels of summary tasks. Then the team can split off into smaller groupings to break down the work involved for the summary tasks. Once this has been completed bring everyone back together to review your findings and work through any issues that may have arisen.

* Use your scope statement and deliverables to identify the top-level summary tasks.

If we refer back once again to our tried and trusted example of the corporate sales event which involves attending trade shows and producing new sales materials, build in summary tasks to cover them. Then, methodically break down the work that goes into each of the summary tasks. This may sound like boring, monotonous work, but it is absolutely essential to keeping your project on track. Having immediate deliverables will pay dividends at this point as they will help you identify lower-level summary tasks. (Signed contracts springs to mind.)

At this point, you need to figure out how much you need to breakdown. You might want to start by breaking down project work to match the frequency of your status reports. Most project managers aim for work packages that take between eight and eighty hours to complete, and you can use the following test to ascertain whether or not you have correctly broken the work down:

- Are time and cost easy to estimate?
- Is status easy to measure?
- Are task durations shorter than your reporting periods?
- Is the detail at a level that you can and crucially *want* to manage?

Different parts of a project might need to be broken down in more depth than others. One part of the project might include more work, so you break it down into three levels, whereas another simpler project might only need two levels. There is no need to worry at this stage about your initial organization of your WBS; there will be plenty of time to review this later to see whether or not you want to rearrange tasks.

Estimating

Getting your cost and timings right is crucial to the overall success of your project. The buck stops with you on this, and it is your job as project manager to make sure that that you get this down to the nearest cent. It is important that you appreciate that both your customer and your sponsor are looking to understand exactly how much time and budget is going to be required before sanctioning a project. Getting this wrong could lead them to question the validity of the project – particularly if you budget too low!

Providing an accurate estimate is not an easy task because even the best estimate may have to be based on an educated guess. As we have already discussed, there are just two things to be estimated in a project: timings and costings. For timings, it is predominantly about people involved and how long they are likely to collectively take to deliver the project in its entirety. However, you should also remember to factor in time associated with equipment hire as well as any travelling that will be needed.

As your estimating is such an important aspect of planning, it goes without saying that you need people you can rely upon to assist you. This is not a task that you would ever be expected to undertake on your own, and in most companies you would work with a project planning team, that was comprised of people who had a working knowledge of the project. The planning team will help you develop initial estimates. If this option is not open to you, then you may want to consider bringing in external specialists.

Later in the process, it will be possible to re-assess the initial estimates and revisit them to create a more accurate picture. This is because the people in place will have a much better idea of their actual work rate and will want to ensure that they are able to deliver on the estimates that they sign up to. However, remember that too much movement in either direction is not good for you, your customer or your sponsor.

Wherever possible you consider the results of similar projects in order to come up with an accurate estimate for a new one. This might seem like common sense, but you would be surprised at how many people neglect to do it. If you are in this position, then you can adopt to use the Parametric model to create your estimate. Put simply, it considers other similar projects that you have completed and then matches them to the new project based on a specific measure. So, for example, if your project involved the construction of a new building, then the model would determine effort and cost based on the number of square feet. All you need to do is plug the numbers into a spreadsheet or program and let technology take care of the rest.

If this option isn't open to you, do not despair as there is another way in which you can reach an accurate estimate, even when starting from scratch. It is known as PERT and it stands for Program Evaluation and Review Technique. By adopting this approach you effectively construct the estimate using three attributes: the best, worst and most likely result, kind of like an averaging process.

If you are not comfortable with the idea of putting the estimate together on your own, then you can, of course, bring in others to provide comparative estimates. This works best if you work with several experienced professional and ask them to provide the estimate independent from one another in order to compare and contrast until you reach a mutual agreement as to the best one to put forward – again using averaging if necessary. This method is quite often referred to as the Delphi Technique.

In using the Delphi Technique, you can choose to just focus on the major attributes of the project and then breakdown the costs further to ascertain the smaller parts right down to the point of individual tasks. This is a good route to take if you are working on a sizeable project. Remember also with projects of this nature, to give further time consideration for any complexities, number of meetings and other interactions as well as travel aspects. The list goes on; but hopefully this gives you the general idea.

For smaller projects, you may find it easier to create your estimate by putting a figure to each of the individual tasks and then summing them up to provide the overall figure.

Whichever method you choose to use, you also need to be aware of any buffers that people may be adding in to give them a bit of a safety net should anything go awry. It is human nature to do this and I found that one of the best ways to mitigate this is to make it publicly known that you will be creating a central buffer of funds to be used as required.

Later, I will talk to you about critical chain management and you will learn that this method does in fact build in a buffer, albeit as a way to deliver the project in a quicker time but more about that later.

I guess what I am trying to say is that whilst estimating is a crucial step, there are a number of methods to help and it all depends on your personal circumstances as to which one you choose. Ultimately you are responsible and once you have made your decision it is then a question of who you want to assist you.

One final word of advice on estimating – always make sure that you have agreed a contingency budget (both in terms of time and money) with the sponsor/customer so that you are in a position to address any issues as they come up – and they will!

Creating Dependencies Between Tasks

Getting your tasks in the correct order is a key part of building a schedule. Tasks are often more closely interlinked, with one task often only able to start after another has finished. Say for example you need to have your sales documents designed before you can print them. By linking tasks, you turn a list of tasks into a sequence that defines when each will occur. Task dependency is when one task controls the timing of others. Because each task has a start and finish, there are four types of task dependencies.

The most common type of dependencies are finish-to-start, with the end of one task controlling when the other task starts. For example, in its most basic sense you have to finish making a flight reservation before someone can get on the plane. By contrast, you have the start-to-start dependencies, where one task triggers the start of another. So for example, when the tradeshow starts your sales team also starts their presentations in the booth.

Start-to-finish dependencies in which the start of one task triggers the finish of another don't occur very often. In this scenario, the task in control occurs after the one it controls. For example, the start of the trade show breakdown determines when sales presentations end, no matter how interested the customers are.

So, how do you decide which type of dependency to run with? Well, you can do this by asking a few simple questions. Which task controls the other? This will tell you which task is the primary one in the dependency. Does the start or finish date of the first task control the second task? This helps you identify whether the dependency begins with the start or finish. Does the first task control the start or finish of the second task? This identifies whether the second half of the dependency is start or finish.

Task dependencies place tasks into a sequence so you can build your project's schedule. So now that you are familiar with the different types, you might want to try and identify all the task dependencies in your project.

Understanding Work, Duration & Units

You want the best people on your project, right? Well in order to achieve that, you need to fully understand the relationship between work, duration and units in order to assign the right people to work on your tasks and get the job ticking over like clockwork. Work, sometimes also called effort, is the number of hours or days someone works on a task. Duration is the length of time between tasks starting and finishing. So, let's run with the following example and assume that you think it will take ten hours of work to print and assemble sales packets which will then be handed out at an event.

If you spend two hours per day, then the duration is five days. If you spend five hours per day, the duration is two days. The work stays the same, but the duration varies. The term for the percentage of time a person spends on a task is often called units. In the project world, units are based on a typical workday--eight hours in a lot of cases. So when someone works full time, eight hours a day, units are 100%.

Okay, so now we need to drill down and look at what happens if you only work two hours per day. Let's do the math! Two hours out of a possible eight hours equates to 25% of each working day. It's like you take a working day and divide it into four pieces. So it is going to take four pieces of the task to make one full day's worth of work. Because you are working 25% of each day, you now have a task that is going to last for four days, and, therefore, your duration is four days.

If you assign more than one person to a task, you still change the units, but the duration, or length of the task will decrease. For example, if we roll again with the same one-day task. Assigning two people to the task will enable them to work simultaneously. That is the same as taking the one day and dividing it into two half-day tasks. By assigning two people to the task, the duration shortens to half a day. However, you need to remember that there are also the tasks that that don't get shorter no matter how many people you assign. Meetings are a classic example of this. A one-day meeting is one day, whether three people attend or ten. Because of the relationship between duration, work, and units, you can assign people in different ways and manipulate the schedule to make it do what you want it to.

Using Milestones

Here's a little history lesson for you! The term Milestones comes from the past when people placed stones by the side of a road to mark each mile. In projects, milestones do a similar job, but they represent progress and other key project points rather than distance. Milestones are great as the first and last tasks in your project's schedule. By starting a project with a milestone, you can easily reschedule the project start date just by moving the starting milestone to a later date. The last task in a project's schedule is almost always a milestone.

Milestones are great because:

- Looking to the final milestone as a reference you can tell whether the project is on time, late or ahead of schedule.
- They highlight progress made between a project's start and finish.
- You get the satisfaction of marking off all the work you have done to date when the milestone is complete.
- Milestones can be used to flag the anticipated delivery of a key aspect of a project.

Making a Realistic Schedule

Using your WBS (as described in the previous sections), you should now be in a position to estimate the time that each element of your project is likely to take – or at least, get very close to it. Once you have an understanding of this, your next task is to assign work to individuals based on how many hours they are going to be giving to the project on any given day. It is important that you get this as accurate as possible to ensure that the project's actual performance is as close to the original plan as possible.

The best place to start is with your full-time workers although you will need to factor in that not ALL of their time is going to be dedicated to your project. With the best will in the world, other areas of their usual 'day job' will undoubtedly creep in. For example, it is likely that they will still be expected to attend departmental meetings, carry out admin tasks and even attend training courses. Let's face it, even a trip across campus or riding the elevator eats into a working day! All you can do is acknowledge this and reduce the time available accordingly to get to an estimate that is a realistic projection of the time available.

The other area to give consideration to and one that quite often gets missed, is the speed at which any given team member works; and this can often be determined by what they have a natural aptitude for. For example, you could have someone with excellent writing skills who can put together engaging presentations and reports in next to no time when compared to those who are more comfortable with numbers. In assessing who to assign which tasks to, it is important to consider this in order to maximize productivity. However, a word of warning – do not allocate more than three tasks to any one individual no matter how tempting it might seem as this will definitely be counter-productive.

After the full-timers, you are then on to any part-time staff, again factoring in any time-depleting factors like you did with the full-time workers and taking into account any particular aptitudes.

Understanding The Critical Path

Within your project there will be two types of tasks; those that have some flexibility and those that don't. The critical path is concerned with the latter and it is these that can make or break a project in terms of both time and budget. I guess that is why they are called 'critical'!

Quite often tasks on the critical path also have the longest duration but not always. They also tend to be at the start of a task sequence which means there is no 'wriggle room' without having a knock on effect on the overall schedule. However, identifying tasks on the critical path is not as simple as it first might seem – let's take a look at a potential example:

So, say the end deliverable is to get some hand-outs to an event and the deadline for delivery is September 15. The tasks involved would be in the simplest of terms to develop handouts, print handouts and ship materials. At first glance, it could look as though all three tasks are on the critical path and there is no identifiable flexibility or slack. However, let's take a closer look:

Let's suppose that the earliest we can develop the handouts is August 10 and the latest is August 20 – already we can see that this task is NOT on the critical path. Now, if we were to achieve the earlier date and get the materials ready for printing before August 20, we would still have to wait to start printing at our agreed print slot of August 20 and as a result both print handouts and ship materials are on the critical path as the dates cannot be moved.

Fortunately, this is not something that you have to work out with manual calculations as there are project scheduling programs that will do this for you. However, it is important to understand the critical path and that its importance is widely communicated.

Understanding The Critical Chain Method

Aside from the critical path, there is also another technique that may be worth getting to grips with although not all project managers use it and it does require some level of research to understand how best to put it into practice. However, it would be remiss of me if I didn't at least make reference to it in this document.

In essence, the critical chain is all about maximizing the time available by scheduling tasks to occur as late as possible and the main benefits of doing this are as follows:

- You won't need to pay out until it absolutely becomes necessary.
- You might be able to deliver the project earlier or ensure it completes on time by preventing potential delays.
- Finally, use of the critical chain method uses limited resources in the most effective way – this is because the critical chain focuses on resource limitation in order to identify the most important tasks that need managing.

Using the critical chain method is like adding shared time to a project because it calculates the overall time need for a sequence of tasks (using the latest possible deadline for each task to create maximum time available) and then converts that into a shared buffer. This can be a much more resourceful way of scheduling a project because only the tasks that require the extra time in reality end up using the buffer available.

Shortening a Schedule

Even with all your meticulous planning, it may become necessary to shorten the project schedule in order to deliver the project ahead of time. In the event of this happening (and it occurs more often than you might think), there are really only two ways to do this successfully and that is to either overlap tasks or throw money at it. As you might expect, they both come with a level of risk so let's explore each one in a little more detail:

The technical term for overlapping tasks is 'fast tracking' and as you might expect it is relatively easy to do although there are some best practices that need to be adhered to, to do it successfully. First of all, you need to decide which tasks can be overlapped with one another and these are usually those on the critical path. The reason for this is that not only do you shorten the overall project schedule, but you reduce the critical path at the same time. However, in taking this approach you need to be mindful that decisions further down the line are not going to affect tasks already completed and lead to increased work and potential costs.

Now we come to the money option and this is known as 'crashing' and involves spending more money on the project than was originally budgeted for in order to shorten the overall schedule and the critical path specifically. Generally speaking an additional investment is made in manpower to increase productivity although that isn't always the case. The important thing here is that it is used to shorten the critical path in the most efficient way possible.

The other thing to consider when choosing this option is that anyone new that you bring in is going to be less productive until they get up to speed and so the crash may not be as effective as it appears on paper. There is also an added down-side in that the people already working on the task are going to have to spend time orienting the new guys – time that would not have been factored into your original schedule.

To help assess the best tasks to crash, it is useful to have a crash table as this will include how much it costs to crash each task as well as the amount of time that will be saved by doing so, with a caveat of the risks mentioned previously.

Whichever method you opt to use, you will need to re-look at the critical path as the tasks that were identified on it previously may not be so under this change of circumstances.

Documenting a Baseline

Now that you have an agreed project plan in place, you will want to ensure that you have a method by which to evaluate progress and project performance. This is known as a baseline and is compiled from your approved documents, agreed budget and schedule. Project scheduling programs normally provide a feature for saving a baseline and everything that you include here will form your change control process. This means that any changes in the baseline will show up as change requests.

There are two aspects to documenting a baseline as follows:

Part 1

Save the baseline version of your plan documents in your project notebook. If and when something changes, you will need to highlight it in a revised version of the relevant baseline document.

Part 2

Baseline the values in your project schedule using the project scheduling program. This will need to include the approved start and finish dates, length of tasks, assigned budget and any other data that you feel is relevant. The scheduling program will then be able to highlight any variances as you record your progress.

CHAPTER 4: RUNNING A PROJECT

Running a Project

Now that you have your plan in place including your baseline so that you are able to evaluate performance, you are now ready to galvanize the troops and starting executing (the plan, not heads!) Your first task will be to start engaging and motivating your team by familiarizing them with the tasks to be carried out and their specific assignments. This is your chance to set the working environment and forge strong relationships from the onset. In the interests of transparency and team-working, you will also need to create an environment whereby all of the project information can be accessed. This documentation will help you carry out two of your key responsibilities as project manager:

Monitoring

We all know the old adage 'fail to plan, plan to fail' but even the most meticulous plans can go awry so don't panic if this happens to you! Provided you have been monitoring all of the data that provides you with the state of the project, you will be in a position to roll with the punches and adapt as required.

Controlling

This is the actual change implementation that you will need to administer should you need to get your project back on track.

Executing a Project

It may be that you have some of your team in place but are yet to fill all of the roles that are required for project success. This is quite common as it is often necessary to look at outside resources in order to garner the skills and experience required. Therefore, procurement of the additional vendors will be your first task in delivering the project.

It is likely that there will already be a procurement process in place as set out by your customer or sponsor which you will need to adhere to. If not, then typically it will start with a request for a proposal (RFP) and this will describe the services or resource you are looking for, the timescales and the allocated budget. It is also worth adding any particular criteria that you expect the vendor to fulfill so that they know whether or not they meet all your requirements before placing a bid.

Once all the bids have been received, you now need to decide who you will go with, and often the easiest way to do this is to create a table of all the vendors and give them a score again each of the criteria that you are judging their bid against. Of course, this assumes that all the criteria carry an equal weighting so it may be necessary to add a weighting factor too. Depending on the size and the complexity of the project, it may even be necessary to create a shortlist of possible vendors and invite them to a formal meeting.

Having selected the resources that best meet your requirements, you will need to draw up a contact that sets out the statement of work, terms and conditions, deliverables, deadlines and the agreed price. In terms of cost, there are several types of contacts and which one you choose will depend on the nature of the project. They are as follows:

Fixed price

As the name implies these are contracts where the vendor is paid a fixed amount for a specific set of deliverables, irrespective of the time and expenses incurred.

Time and materials

Again the clue is in the name! These pay based on the time worked and the expenses incurred.

Cost plus

This is the same as time and materials with the added element of a fee penalty or reward depending on the performance of the vendor.

Retainer

A specified amount of time is paid for upfront and the ongoing work is defined as the project progresses.

Of the four, the contacts relating to time and materials present the most risk to the project and to minimize this I recommend that you include a not-to-exceed-a- value clause.

With all your team now in place, you have reached the stage where you want to bring them all together and get things moving…. The key thing here being motivation, motivation, motivation!

It is a good idea to bring in the sponsors and the customer at this stage and let them open the session by describing the mission and showing just how behind it they are. It also goes along way if they personally welcome and thank all the team for their involvement. Also, as it is unlikely that everyone will already know each other, as the project manager, it is a good idea to have an ice breaker or two ready in order to set the tone for interaction and co-operative working.

This is also a good time for you to share the detail of the project plan as well as the working processes that you would like everyone to follow – start as you mean to go on. I have already talked about the need for a central accessible place for project information and this should be shared also – preferably with details on a hand-out so that you don't get people asking you where the project notebook is stored because they have forgotten what you said. Trust me, a little bit of hand-holding at this stage will avoid headaches further down the line!

Understanding Team Dynamics

In any instance when you bring a group of people together and call them a 'team' it takes a little while for them to gel. However, you want to speed up this process as much as possible in order to reach the high-performance levels that you inevitably going to need in order to deliver the project. One way to do this is to understand the transitions that your team need to go through in order to reach that level and I think Bruce Tuckman describes it best:

Forming – Stage 1

This is when the team members are coming together for the first time. They are talking about why they are here, what are they doing, what is their goal? what is their purpose? During this stage, as a leader you have to keep everyone focused on the goals and make sure that everyone understands them.

Storming – Stage 2

This is when the conflict starts to happen. Here what you have is different people going in different directions. No one much and it can feel pretty chaotic. If you are lucky, then you will get through storming and on to the next stage. As a leader, this is the best time for you to focus defining on roles and strategies. This way, everyone is fighting about the right thing and you don't deteriorate into bickering or arguing.

Norming – Stage 3

Typically a group can only reach this stage if they have already established their goals. People are starting to go in same direction and starting to see some output. By this point, the team should be experiencing strong unit cohesion; this can be reinforced a great deal just by keeping the ball rolling. Communication is the key here, and a good Project Manager must spend time in developing his or her signature working style and processes.

Performing – Stage 4

This is when everyone is finally working with ease and have a clear idea of the overall goal of a project. This is when everyone is on the same page and has a shared vision. Work is done at a fairly high level of collaboration and effectiveness. Synergy is visible in accomplishing goals and finishing various tasks. Results are expected to be satisfying and problems are solved as a team. At this stage, the team should establish their own unique identity and have a group camaraderie. The team requires delegated tasks from the Project Manager but does not need to be assisted. The project management should be ready to delegate and oversee.

Managing Team Resources

As discussed previously, one of your key responsibilities as project manager is the continued motivation of your team. I have already mapped out the four stages of team development and now I am going to look at some of the tried and tested techniques that you can adopt to ensure that your team operate as a *team* throughout the duration of your project:

- Wherever and whenever possible, quantify the goals and roles that you have set for each member of the team and for yourself.
- When giving feedback, always criticize in private but praise in public. Providing positive feedback in front of peers can amplify the motivation effect, likewise criticizing in private can reduce the negative impact.
- Facilitate interaction among your team as studies show that when a set of individuals identifies as a group, productivity rises.
- Lead by example by demonstrating the ideals that you would your team to convey. This can be as simple as being truthful, even if it leads to a difficult conversation.
- Be supportive and remove obstacles that are preventing team members from carrying out their tasks, wherever possible.
- Show your team the respect they deserve and in doing so invite them to give you feedback on how you are doing and ensure you act upon it.
- Ensure there is open and regular communication between sub-teams as well as the whole team. Set up regular meetings where you can share progress against the baseline and in doing so, encourage ownership.

It is inevitable that problems are going to arise but it is how you handle them that will be of greater importance. It may be that a team member isn't performing at the level you need them to and the solution may be to replace them. However, before you do, take a look at some of the other options first – could they be trained? Is there a communication barrier that needs addressing? Could you extend the time for that particular task? It is often easier to fix the problem than chase it away; particularly when you consider the time and effort that may be required to bed someone else in.

The skills associated with leadership cannot be under-estimated and are fundamental to the success of a project manager. By utilizing the techniques above, you will have a strong foundation from which to build effective working relationships that will ensure successful delivery of your project.

Gathering Data

Once work begins on your project, you need to be constantly kept in the loop about what has already been done and what there is still left to do so that you can be certain that your project is progressing according to plan. The data you need depends on what the customer and other stakeholders consider important and although every project and client are different, schedule and budget usually top the list. Therefore you can guarantee that you are going to need information about hours worked, and money spent:

- Find out when each task has started. A task might only take the work hours you estimated, but if it starts two weeks late, it could delay your project.
- Gather actual work hours, or in some cases, duration. Tracking hours worked takes more effort and is laborious, but it will give you a clearer picture of task progress and the labor costs associated with the work.
- Find out how much work or time is remaining. This will not only tell you how much longer a task will run, but also whether or not your original estimate was on target. If possible, set up an automated way of obtaining the information you need about tasks, such as e-mail, a web form, or an enterprise-wide project- status reporting tool.

Evaluating Progress

Once you've collected the data that you need from your team, the fun begins, and you can begin to evaluate the progress of your project. A good project manager will always look at their project from several different angles in order to uncover and resolve problems.

1. Examine the project's schedule, because delays can lead to other problems. Compare the current schedule to your original plan. A Gantt chart is a brilliant means of identifying whether tasks are ahead of, behind or bang on target. It does this by showing your original baseline schedule with bars in one color and your current schedule with another color and is, therefore, simple but effective.
2. Variance values show you the exact difference between your baseline and your current schedule. It's helpful to hone in on problem tasks. If you use a scheduling program, there are often filters and views that provide early warnings of delays.
3. Then, look at cost. Cost issues can arise if tasks take more hours to complete than have been allocated. Increases in the cost can also occur due to higher resource costs or paying overtime. Cost variances show the difference between your baseline costs and the current scheduled costs.

Understanding Earned Value Analysis

Earned value analysis will show you how much a project has earned based on work that's been completed, or, to put it another way, a project earns true value when work is completed. You need to understand how deceptive basic project measures can be in order to understand fully and appreciate earned value. Let us imagine that half of the time allocated for your project has elapsed. Half of the budget has been spent. You might assume that you were bang on target. However, if only around a quarter of the work has been completed, then you might run into difficulties.

You still have three-quarters left to complete, but with only half of the time allocation and half of the money, you are never in a month of Sundays going to pull this one out of the bag. Earned value analysis will unearth this while you still have a chance to do something about it. It offers up your schedule and budget as pure hard cash. This can be quite an eye-opener as you will get to see the performance of your project in the same units. Yes, costs have a monetary value; but this little beauty enables you to measure work as if it were cash by working out how much it would cost for your staff to undertake the work.

Earned value analysis is based on three things:

1. Planned value. (Budgeted cost of work scheduled) How much you plan to spend in order to complete the work.
2. Earned value is the amount of cash that you received upon completing the work.
3. The final cost for the completed work.

Putting this all into a graph and analyzing it is an old school but incredibly effective way of checking that your project is in budget and on time. Imagine your graph is on the wall. This is how you would read it:

- The horizontal axis contains time.

- The vertical axis houses cost.
- Planned value needs to be below-earned value (Yay, you are ahead of schedule! Big bonus for you!)
- Earned value should be higher than costs (Yay, you've spent less than budget! Extra big bonus for you!)

Reporting On Progress

Remember earlier when I mentioned that interpersonal skills were core to your role as a project manager? When you are not analyzing data, then communication is the name of your game. A reporting system will help ensure that you communicate with the right people on time, every time. Having a decent reporting system gives you the ability to gather accurate information in a timely manner without making a pain in the butt. You have already identified your audiences via your communication plan. Now it is time to communicate!

It is usually enough to collect information from your team on a weekly basis. You could request status updates midweek with a view to producing reports by the weekend. Once you have your reports, you will then distribute them to your target audience using your method of choice.

Status reports should cover the following:

- Outlining what has happened
- The work that was scheduled
- Work completed
- Anything that went awry.

You should accurately report anything that is slightly out of kilter, and advise the steps you intend to take to correct them. The management team might require a cumulative status report so that they can have an accurate overview of the bigger picture. Dashboards are an excellent and effective means of flagging any issues using the stoplight system.

1. Green for everything is on track
2. Yellow for minor hiccups
3. Red for major problems

Understanding Financial Measures

Now, I am going to walk you through some of the frequently used financial measures favored by large organizations in order to evaluate the performance of their projects. This is a brilliant way of ensuring that you are meeting the expectations of the management team and stakeholders.

* Capital budgeting analysis examine return on investment (ROI)

Once your schedule is in place, then you will be aware of projected costs and timing. Funding, as we have already mentioned, usually, comes from whoever proposes or approves the project. The time it takes for them to recoup their money can vary. For arguments sake, let's imagine that a project cost $100,000 and generates sales of $10,000 per month. In this instance, ROI would be ten months.

ROI runs on the principle that the project will continue making long enough to recoup all of the outlay. That is not always the case, and NPV, or Net present value is a more accurate measure as it uses the time value of money. Inflationary pressures can wreak havoc with your budget. So it is a good idea to set a target rate for ROI and use NPV to figure out whether your project exceeds, meets or falls short of the target return.

You also need to familiarize yourself with the internal rate of return (IRR.) Rather than a month by month analysis, this shows the annual return and factors in the time value of money. It is similar to the annual percentage yield that you earn on savings in your bank account.

Communicating Effectively

We have already discussed the importance of excellent interpersonal skills. You already know that as project manager you are going to be expected to communicate with people at all different levels. Effective and smart communication isn't about being bossy or arrogant; it is about ensuring that the person you are communicating with understands your message and actions it. This will help your teams overall productivity, which in turn will help keep your project flowing.

- Communicate clearly
- Don't waffle, get straight to the point
- Remember that you are a chameleon, therefore you need to tailor your message to your audience. Use language that is non-threatening and that they understand.
- Positivity will get you a long way
- If there is a problem be clear about it and what you intend to do about it.

Good communication is an art form. No-one is born a great communicator; it is a skill that we learn over time.

- Listening is as important as talking. A manager who never listens does not have their people's ear, and this can lead to a whole host of avoidable miscommunications
- If someone is talking to you give them your full attention – It is rude not to!
- Switch off your cell phone. Easier said than done, I know.
- If you are meeting with them in person then observe body language. It is amazing how much you can learn about the true state of your project by watching people's facial expressions.
- Constantly check your understanding by repeating or paraphrasing back what you have heard. This not only is effective for communication, but it will also help build a rapport and establish trust.
- Remember email is for work, not for pleasure. Make effective use of it and keep conversations about what happened at the weekend for outside of working hours. Email is a

quick and easy method of communications but is not without its pitfalls as messages can be ambiguous and misunderstood. Treat email in the same way, that you would a normal conversation. Be clear and concise in the delivery of your message. Always proofread your messages. Yes, it is time-consuming but spelling mistakes and grammatical errors can drastically change the meaning of a message. Remember that your emails are a virtual manifestation of you. Treat them with respect! Good communication like a good marriage requires work. Remember this and you won't go far wrong!

Running Meetings Effectively

Meetings can be a major time sink unless handled with care. Meetings involve numerous people, they are costly, and they are frequently abused; used as a chance to catch up on social events. Love them or hate them, meetings are sometimes the most effective way of banging heads together and getting things done. Make your meetings count. You can use an agenda to make sure you cover every item, keep the discussion on the topic, and to finish for meeting on time. On your agenda list the topics to discuss. Include your time estimate for each topic. The more people you have in a meeting the harder it is to get things done. The third step is to limit the attendees to the people you need to accomplish your goal. Fourth, give attendees a chance to prepare.

- Know what you want to achieve and go into it with a clear agenda.
- Don't be a brat. Schedule the meeting for a time that works for the majority of attendees, rather than for yourself.
- Give plenty of advance notice.
- Ensure that they start and finish on time.
- Don't make the mistake of recapping if people turn up late
- Get someone to take detailed notes so that you can formally document decisions reached.

Getting A Project Back On Track

Even with the best will in the world, something is going to go wrong with your project at some point. Being a project manager is a bit like being a trapeze artist at a circus. You will constantly find yourself juggling scope schedule, cost, and quality. In this section, I am going to walk you through how to make effective changes speedily and with minimal impact.

- Think about the things that you can do without seeking permission from a higher level. Action them.
- If you have to go higher up the food chain, ask stakeholders for their consent. For example, you may need to lengthen the schedule, increase the budget, etc. Be armed with pros and cons and be ready to set out your stall and fight your corner.
- If you are working for a large organization, you may have to go higher up the corporate ladder. This often happens if you need to divert manpower from other projects, or if you need to tap into contingency funds. If you have a reputation for managing your projects efficiently, then you will have a greater chance of getting the approval that you seek.

Managing Change, Risk, & Quality

During the planning process, you spent hours creating plans for managing changes, risks, and quality. So now that your project is underway it is time to start stepping up to the plate. It is time to start managing the changes, dealing with the risks and ensuring that quality is always at the forefront of everyone's minds.

- Follow your management plan to letter when the first change requests come in.
- Keep a log of all change requests so that you can monitor and track them.

Like storm clouds, risks frequently blow over without causing any damage. Other times, like bolts of lightning, risks appear out of nowhere and wreak havoc. Think of yourself as the emergency responders, launching an immediate response to each and every risk, no matter how big or small.

Quality control is essential to the effective running of any project. If you run an analysis and discover that quality levels are not what you would expect, then you need to take immediate action to resolve it. Even when your results are of the required standard, you still need to keep monitoring.

CHAPTER 5: CLOSING A PROJECT

Closing A Project

Okay, so you have made it to the end, and you have handed over the last of the deliverables. Job done, right? No. There are still several tasks that you need to perform before you can sign this beauty off.

1. First, your customer needs to agree that the project has been completed to their satisfaction.
2. Lessons learned need to be documented so that mistakes are not repeated on future projects.
3. You need to produce final documentation and a closing report.
4. Then you will need to close the contracts, file away any paperwork and reassign your staff.

Gaining Customer Acceptance

You can't sign off on a project without customer approval. Again, this might sound like stating the obvious, however, unless you have a signed piece of paper, confirming that they are happy, then the job simply isn't done. You should be armed and primed with the deliverables that you have documented, as well as your definition of success criteria. You now need to measure that success, and prove beyond doubt that you have ticked all of the required boxes.

Documenting Lessons Learned

Just like life lessons, learning lessons from your project can help you grow and evolve as a project manager, and can make each new project seem more enlightening than the last. With vital lessons under your belt, you will go on to bigger and more complex projects. Everyone likes to sing their own praises from time to time and acknowledging that there were even any problems at all can sometimes seem like a bitter pill to swallow. Be careful not to offend anyone, or hurt anyone's pride. Coax this vital information out of your team members by any means possible.

Don't make the mistake of waiting right until the end of a project and then just dumping this on them, as apart from the fact that you might seriously be bursting their euphoric bubble, they might also have forgotten several key details along the way! Make time in your weekly status meetings for this task. Make it seem natural, and the information will flow naturally.

- Be positive
- Turn negatives into a joke
- See the humor in depressing situations
- Encourage honesty even when you don't like what you are hearing. A suggestion box can be a great way of breaking down this barrier. It is also a brilliant way of dealing with sensitive issues, or when people are reluctant to admit to making mistakes, or are fearful for their jobs. Put yourself in their shoes and try and see things through their eyes.

Preparing A Close-Out Report & Archiving

Part of the closing process is preparing a closeout report, or in other words a final status report. This should succinctly and smoothly sum up the project in an informative and concise document. It should include things such as:

- What the project achieved
- How successful it was
- You should spell out the one thing that the client wants to hear in the opening line:
- Was the project a success?
- This should not be relegated to a yes or no answer. You have spent months building to this moment, so elaborate. Spell it out in all its gory glory.
- Next, include the final cost of the whole project. Stakeholders are very eager to have this information, and there is nothing to be gained from burying it deep with the report.
- Document the delivery dates for the entire project as well as key milestones. If the project was significantly early or late, include the variances from your original dates give the reasons as to why.

Highlight risks that occurred and the steps that you have taken to overcome them. This your moment in the spotlight to shine, make full use of it without appearing arrogant or pompous. Point out risks that occurred that were not previously identified will help prevent others from falling foul in the future.

- End with a detailed analysis of the effectiveness of the management processes within your project. Outline what went well and the things you would recommend doing differently in the future.
- Archive information electronically, this will make it a lot easier for others to find later on.

Closing Contracts, Accounts & Transitioning

There are always annoying little tidbits that need tidying up at the end of any project. Ignoring them looks messy and will not reflect well on you. Here is a checklist of the things that you will need to do:

- Close any open contracts. Remember you will need that crucial signature from your client. Confirm that all contractors have fulfilled their obligations.
- You may also need to support any remaining deliverables.
- Follow up in a few months.
- Close any accounts that you have used. You may need to keep the financial books open for a short time in order to follow up on expenses, etc.
- Close all accounting codes except ones related to follow ups. This will prevent people abusing your generosity.
- Help your team move to new assignments.

Yay, your project is now complete...Next!

CONCLUSION

What's Next?

My main goal in putting together this book was to cover the major processes of project management and effectively explain in layman's terms the many techniques that can be adopted. There are, however many more sources of information that those with an inquisitive mind and thirst for learning can turn to.

Project Management Institute (PMI) is a top notch not-for-profit professional membership association for the project, program and portfolio management profession.

PMI offers many levels of certification, such as the project management professional or PMP. In order to obtain your certification, you have to have a number of hours of experience, complete accredited training, and pass a certification exam. There is another project management methodology known as Prince2, which is based in U.K. The Prince2.com website has a bunch of training material as well as certification opportunities.

Many schools now offer certificates and degrees in project management. You can look up several accredited degree programs in project management on the PMI website. I recommend that you apply the skills you've learned from this book and then in a few months, come back and revisit all these concepts. You will find that becoming an accomplished project manager is a learning experience that can last a lifetime.

About The Author

Fareed Raja is a writer, traveler, and a project professional. He is a big fan of consumer behavior and spent majority of his professional years in sales and project management. He likes to refer to himself in the third person #illeism. And he also started using hashtags more recently #hashtags.

After getting his MBA from Spring Hill College, he moved to Woodbridge, Virginia and spends most of his time travelling internationally and working with some amazing professionals.

He speaks four languages and his new found love is teaching virtually on a number of subjects. Don't forget to connect with him on LinkedIn, Twitter, and Udemy. Also if you enjoyed this book, feel free to download more. Click here to go to his Amazon author page.

https://linkedin.com/in/fareedraja

https://twitter.com/FareedRAhmed

https://udemy.com/u/fareedraja/

www.ingramcontent.com/pod-product-compliance
Lightning Source LLC
Chambersburg PA
CBHW070845180526
45168CB00002B/958